Solar System Superstar

About Wise & Wide

- A systematic 6-level English reading program based on Lexile® measures
- Diverse and interesting topics chosen from the elementary curriculums of Korea and English speaking western countries
- Well-written books in various forms including fiction stories, descriptive texts, and classics retold
- The informative but original fiction stories grab your interest, leading to the easy and clear understanding of the educational content.
- Improve thinking skills with solid after-reading activities at all levels of the series.

Wise & Wide is a 6-level English reading program that consists of 60 books and each level is systematically divided by Lexile® measures. The Lexile® Framework for Reading is the most popular reading measuring system in American formal education curriculums and many English programs. Over 20 out of 50 states in the U.S. mark Lexile® measures directly on students' final report cards and over 300 well-known publishers adopt and use Lexile® measures.

Experience many kinds of readings written by professional writers from the U.S. and England. They used interesting topics that were carefully chosen after analyzing elementary curriculums from around the world including Korea, the U.S., England, and Australia among many others. Comprehensive after-reading activities including graphic organizers, speaking tasks, and After-reading Tests are ready for you.

Levels in the series and their corresponding Lexile® measures

Level	Lexile® measures	U.S. Grade
Level 1	Below 200L	Pre K - K
Level 2	190L - 400L	Lower Grade 1
Level 3	350L - 530L	Upper Grade 1
Level 4	420L - 650L	Grade 2
Level 5	520L - 940L	Grade 3 - 4
Level 6	830L - 1070L	Grade 5 - 6

* Smart Readers: Wise & Wide level 1 is applicable to the preschool level in the U.S.
* The source of the relationship between Lexile® measures and U.S. school grades: CCSS(Common Core State Standards) FOR ENGLISH LANGUAGE ARTS, APPENDIX A (2012, which is used by 45 states in the U.S.)

Topic List

	Level 1	Level 2	Level 3	Level 4	Level 5	Level 6
Book 1	Science>Biology: The hibernation of animals Story	Science>Biology: Living and nonliving things Story	Science>Biology> Animals & the Environment: Sea otters Story	Environment> Living with nature: The diver & the persimmon tree Story	Science>Biology> Animal Amazing animals of the Amazon Story	Science>Biology: Germs, transmitted diseases Story
Book 2	Literature> World classics: Aesop's fables Story	Literature> Traditional fairy tale: Old tales about stones Story	Social Studies> Economy: To run a business to make and save money Story	Science>Biology> Plants: Photosynthesis Story	Science>Earth science: Earth's layers, earthquakes, volcanoes, and earth's atmosphere Report	Mathematics> Sequence: The golden ratio & the Fibonacci sequence Story
Book 3	Science>Physics: How shadows are formed Story	Literature> World classics: Peter Pan Story	Science>Scientific technology: Nanobots Story	Literature>Myths: World's creation stories Story	Literature> Legend: The story of King Arthur Story	Literature>Myths: Constellation myths Story
Book 4	Literature> Traditional literature: The Talmud Story	Science>Biology> Animal: Polar bears Story	Science>Biology> Animal: Mountain gorillas Story	Social Studies> Cultural anthropology: Amazing ancient cultures of the world Story	Science> Earth science: Clouds and weather Story	Literature> Human & animals: The friendship between a girl and a horse Story
Book 5	Social Studies> Ethics: Rules in daily life Story	Science>Biology: The five senses Report	Social Studies> Cultural anthropology: Astonishing festivals Report	Art>Music: Stories from two operas Story	Social Studies> World culture & history: The Renaissance Story	Sports> Board sports: Surfing & snowboarding Story
Book 6	Social Studies> World geography & travel: Tourist attractions around the world Story	Science>Biology> Animal: Dinosaurs Story	Science> Astronomy: The solar system Story	Social Studies> People: Three great people who overcame hardships Story	Science>Scientific technology: The wonderful world of robots Report	Art>Music: Composers of the Romantic Era Report
Book 7	Science> Space science: The life of astronauts Report	Social Studies> Cultural anthropology: Mythological monsters from around the world Report	Mathematics> Elementary mathematics: Numbers, measurement, shapes and data Report	Science & Social Studies> Technology & culture: Inventions from around the world Report	Art>Works of art: Famous paintings Report	Social Studies> Human & animals: Animals in action for human Report
Book 8	Social Studies> Cultural anthropology: Various living cultures of the world Story	Art>Music: Instruments in the orchestra Story		Social Studies> History: The California Gold Rush Report	Social Studies & Science> Psychology: Psychology in everyday life Story	Literature> World classics: The Merchant of Venice Story
Book 9						
Book 10						

* 10 books in each level will be published.

How to Use
This Book

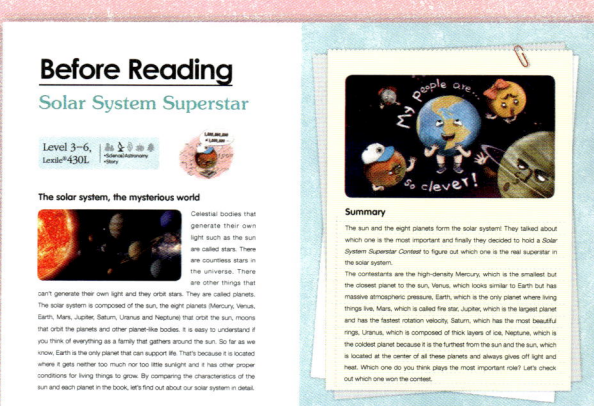

• Before Reading

You can easily find the topic and what kind of story you are about to read.

• The text

All the stories were written by professional writers from the U.S. and England, so you will read authentic and appropriate English sentences and expressions in every book in the series.

• Pop Quiz

Check out right away if you understand what you have just read by solving a pop quiz that checks your comprehension.

• Key Words

The key words and expressions on each page are listed for you to easily study them.

• Aha! Tips

Download free Korean explanations at *www.ihappyhouse.co.kr* for all of the sentences marked with "Aha!". These explain cultural, scientific, and economic knowledge or they deal with aspects of English such as grammatical structures or idiomatic expressions. There are lots of "Aha! Tips" to help you understand the text.

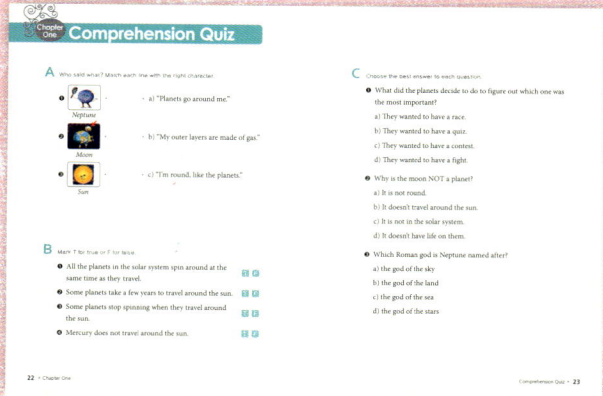

•Comprehension Quiz

After reading one chapter, solve various questions to find out if you fully understand the content.

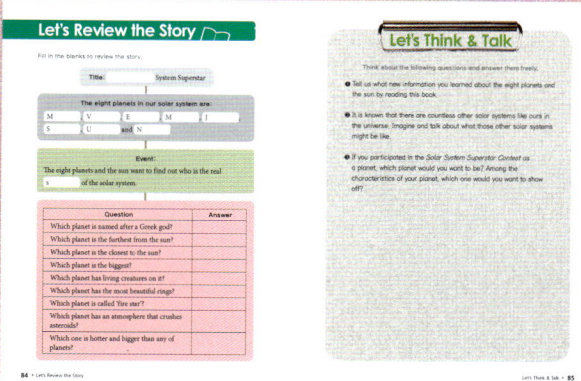

•Let's Review the Story /
•Let's Think & Talk

Fill in the blanks in the organizer to summarize the whole story. Express your own thinking and feelings about the story by answering the questions. You can build up logic and reasoning skills for your essay examinations in the future.

Appendix

Audio CD

In the CD audio book form, the texts are read vividly by American professional voice actors. (MP3 files downloaded for free)

After-reading Test

Solve an additionally provided After-reading Test for each book.

The Korean translation, Answer Keys, a Word Quiz, a Word List, and Aha! Tips for each book

You can download them for free at *www.ihappyhouse.co.kr* or *www.darakwon.co.kr*

Before Reading

Solar System Superstar

Level 3–6,
Lexile® 430L

•Science〉Astronomy
•Story

1,000,000,000 × 1,000,000 ....

The solar system, the mysterious world

Celestial bodies that generate their own light such as the sun are called stars. There are countless stars in the universe. There are other things that can't generate their own light and they orbit stars. They are called planets. The solar system is composed of the sun, the eight planets (Mercury, Venus, Earth, Mars, Jupiter, Saturn, Uranus and Neptune) that orbit the sun, moons that orbit the planets and other planet-like bodies. It is easy to understand if you think of everything as a family that gathers around the sun. So far as we know, Earth is the only planet that can support life. That's because it is located where it gets neither too much nor too little sunlight and it has other proper conditions for living things to grow. By comparing the characteristics of the sun and each planet in the book, let's find out about our solar system in detail.

Summary

The sun and the eight planets form the solar system! They talked about which one is the most important and finally they decided to hold a *Solar System Superstar Contest* to figure out which one is the real superstar in the solar system.

The contestants are the high-density Mercury, which is the smallest but the closest planet to the sun, Venus, which looks similar to Earth but has massive atmospheric pressure, Earth, which is the only planet where living things live, Mars, which is called fire star, Jupiter, which is the largest planet and has the fastest rotation velocity, Saturn, which has the most beautiful rings, Uranus, which is composed of thick layers of ice, Neptune, which is the coldest planet because it is the furthest from the sun and the sun, which is located at the center of all these planets and always gives off light and heat. Which one do you think plays the most important role? Let's check out which one won the contest.

Contents

Solar System Superstar

Solar System Superstar

Chapter One

Neptune Begins the Contest

One day, the sun looked at the planets around it.

There were eight planets.

Each planet traveled around the sun.

Around and around they went.

Some of them took a few months to travel around the sun.

Some of them took a few years.

But they never stopped traveling, around and around.

At the same time, each planet was spinning.

KEY WORDS

- **Neptune**
- **begin** (begin-began-begun)
- **contest**
- **one day**
- **look at**
- **planet**
- **each**
- **travel around** (*cf.* travel)

- **go around and around** (go-went-gone)
- **take** (take-took-taken)
- **a few**
- **month**
- **never**
- **stop + *Verb*-ing**
- **at the same time**
- **spin** (spin-spun-spun)

The names of the planets were: Mercury, Venus, Earth,
Mars, Jupiter, Saturn, Uranus and Neptune.

"Why do we do this?"

Mercury called out to the sun.

"Why do we go around you, Sun?"

"Because I am the most important," laughed the sun.

KEY WORDS

- Mercury
- Venus
- Earth
- Mars
- Jupiter
- Saturn

- Uranus
- call out to
- because
- most
- important
- laugh

- agree
- moon
- argue with
- must + *Verb*
- too
- That's why ~ (*cf.* why)

The planets did not agree.

Most of the planets had some moons.

The moons went around and around their planet.

The planets began to argue with the sun.

"We must be important, too," said Saturn.

"That's why our moons go around and around us."

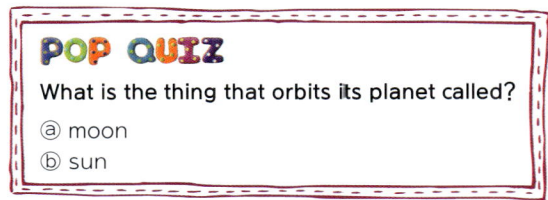

POP QUIZ

What is the thing that orbits its planet called?

ⓐ moon

ⓑ sun

"Let's have a contest," said Jupiter.

"Let's find out who is the real
superstar of the solar system.
We will see who is the
most important."
"A contest," said the sun.
"What a good idea!
Who will go first?"
"Wait," said the beautiful moon
that went around Earth.
"Can I join in the contest?
Can the other moons join in?"

KEY WORDS

- have a contest
- find out (find-found-found)
- real
- superstar
- solar system
- see (see-saw-seen)
- idea
- go first
- wait
- can + *Verb*

- join in
- other
- kindly
- round
- like
- explain
- instead
- so
- disappointed
- have to + *Verb*

"You're not a planet," said the sun, kindly.

"But why not?" asked the moon.

"I'm round, like the planets."

"Planets go around me," explained the sun.

"You go around Earth instead.

So you're not a real planet."

The moon was disappointed, but had to agree.

"Neptune, you're the furthest away from me," called the sun.

"Why don't you go first? Aha!

Tell us why you should be the winner."

"I am so beautiful," boasted Neptune.

"I am blue.

I am named after the Roman god of the sea.

It looks as though I am made of water, but I am not."

KEY WORDS

- furthest
- away from
- call
- why don't you ~?
- tell (tell-told-told)
- should + *Verb*
- winner
- boast
- name after
- Roman
- god
- as though

- be made of
- then
- neighbor
- outer layer (*cf.* layer)
- gas
- below
- thick
- go on
- huge
- more than (*cf.* than)
- across
- quickly

"Then what are you made of?" asked Uranus, Neptune's neighbor.

"My outer layers are made of gas," said Neptune.

The other planets laughed.

"Below the gas is a very thick layer of ice."

Neptune went on.

"I am huge!

I am more than 49,000 km across.

But I can spin quickly."

"You look very cold," said Mercury, who stayed close to the hot sun.

"Are you the coldest planet?"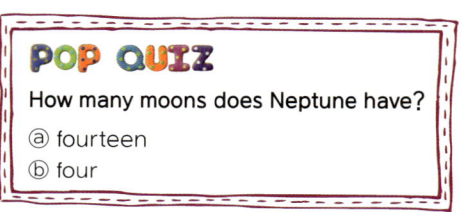

"I think so," said Neptune.

"My surface temperature is around -200˚C."

"Brrr! That really is cold!" said Mercury.

"It's because you're so far away from the sun."

"I have fourteen moons," Neptune went on.

"They go around and around me.

All my moons have names.

The biggest one is called Triton."

POP QUIZ

How many moons does Neptune have?

ⓐ fourteen

ⓑ four

KEY WORDS

- stay
- close to
- coldest
- I think so.

- surface
- temperature
- around
- ˚C(Celsius)

- brrr
- really
- far away
- biggest

Neptune smiled proudly at Triton.

"Tell them why you are so special."

"All moons go around their planet," Triton explained.

"When you go around and around something, there's a special name for it.

It is called 'orbiting.' Aha!

Most moons orbit their planet in the same direction as the planet spins.

I orbit Neptune in the opposite direction from the way it spins."

The other planets were impressed.

"So you can see that I am the most important planet," said Neptune.

"I don't agree.

I am the most important planet," boasted Uranus.

"Let me take my turn at telling you why."

KEY WORDS

- smile at
- proudly
- special
- something

- orbiting
- orbit
- direction
- in the opposite

- impressed
- let (let-let-let)
- take one's turn (*cf.* turn)

A Who said what? Match each line with the right character.

❶
Neptune

❷
Moon

❸
Sun

• a) "Planets go around me."

• b) "My outer layers are made of gas."

• c) "I'm round, like the planets."

B Mark T for true or F for false.

❶ All the planets in the solar system spin around at the same time as they travel. T F

❷ Some planets take a few years to travel around the sun. T F

❸ Some planets stop spinning when they travel around the sun. T F

❹ Mercury does not travel around the sun. T F

C Choose the best answer to each question.

❶ What did the planets decide to do to figure out which one was the most important?

a) They wanted to have a race.

b) They wanted to have a quiz.

c) They wanted to have a contest.

d) They wanted to have a fight.

❷ Why is the moon NOT a planet?

a) It is not round.

b) It doesn't travel around the sun.

c) It is not in the solar system.

d) It doesn't have life on them.

❸ Which Roman god is Neptune named after?

a) the god of the sky

b) the god of the land

c) the god of the sea

d) the god of the stars

Uranus and Saturn

"You certainly have a strange name, Uranus," laughed Neptune.

"We are all named after Roman gods, but I've never heard of Uranus."

Uranus frowned at them all.

"My name makes me special.

All of you, except Earth, are named after Roman gods.

I am named after the Greek god of the sky."

KEY WORDS

- certainly
- strange
- hear of (hear-heard-heard)
- frown at
- except
- Greek

- be full of
- giggle
- scientist
- giant
- core
- center

"You're full of gas, like Neptune," giggled Mercury.

"That is true," agreed Uranus.

"But scientists call me an ice giant.

My outer layers are made of gas. Aha!

Below them is a very thick layer of ice.

My core is the very center of me.

It is made of ice and rock."

"That's all very impressive," said Neptune, "but you can't be as cold as me." Aha!

"It's true that my surface is not as cold as yours," said Uranus.

"But my atmosphere is colder.

It's -224°C."

"Atmosphere?

What's an atmosphere?" asked Mercury.

"Do I have one of those?"

"It's the layer of gases around me," explained Uranus.

POP QUIZ

Which planet has the colder surface?

ⓐ Neptune
ⓑ Uranus

KEY WORDS

- impressive
- atmosphere
- colder
- storm
- such

- interesting
- in amazement
- jealous
- may + *Verb*
- how many + *Plural noun*

"The gases spin around with me.
There are clouds and storms in my atmosphere.
I am such an interesting planet!"
The other planets looked at Uranus in amazement.
But Neptune was jealous.
"You may be colder than me, but how many moons
do you have?"
Uranus smiled.
"Twenty-seven moons."

Neptune scowled.

"Do they have names?"

"Yes, they do.

They are named after characters from the plays of Shakespeare. **Aha!**

He was a writer from Earth, you know."

Earth smiled proudly, and said, "My people are so clever!"

"What sort of names?" squeaked Mercury.

"One is called Oberon," said Uranus.

"He is the king of the fairies.

Another of my moons is named after the queen of the fairies."

"Fairy moons!" gasped Venus.

"How beautiful!"

KEY WORDS

- scowl
- character
- play
- Shakespeare
- writer
- know (know-knew-known)
- clever

- sort of
- squeak
- Oberon
- fairy
- another
- gasp

"Have you finished?" snapped Neptune.

"Are there any more amazing facts to tell us?"

"One last thing," said Uranus.

"I am not just a round ball like you, Neptune.

There are thirteen rings around me.

They are made of dust and rocks.

Scientists think that I once had another moon.

It broke into pieces.

Those pieces still orbit me.

They formed the rings around me.

They must love me.

They don't want to leave!"

POP QUIZ

Which planet has rings like Uranus?

ⓐ Saturn
ⓑ Earth

KEY WORDS

- finish
- snap
- amazing
- fact
- last
- ring
- dust

- think (think-thought-thought)
- once
- break into pieces (break-broke-broken)
- still
- form
- leave (leave-left-left)

"If we're talking about rings," interrupted Saturn, "then I am the most important."

All the planets turned towards Saturn.

"You do look amazing," they agreed.

"You look different than all of us."

Saturn smiled.

"My rings spread wide around me."

"How many rings do you have?" asked Uranus.

"Nobody knows exactly how many I have," boasted Saturn.

"There are more than thirty.

They stretch out for over 120,000 km on each side of me."

"They are so beautiful," murmured Venus.

"I love beautiful things."

"What are your rings made of, Saturn?" asked Uranus.

"They are made of chunks of ice and dust," said Saturn.

"Your rings are certainly better than anyone else's rings," said Jupiter.

KEY WORDS

- **spread** (spread-spread-spread)
- **wide**
- **nobody**
- **exactly**
- **stretch out**
- **over**

- on each side
- murmur
- chunk of
- better
- anyone else

"Yes, but how many moons do you have?" shouted
Neptune.

"Fourteen, like me?"

"Or twenty-seven, like me?" laughed Uranus.

Saturn spent a long time counting.

"It's difficult to say exactly how many there are," said
Saturn at last. Aha!

one.two.three

"I have around 150 moons and moonlets in total."

"Moonlets?" said the other planets.

"What are they?"

"They are little moons," said Saturn.

"They're very cute."

"I don't think that's enough to make you the winner," said Jupiter.

"Are there any more interesting facts about you?"

POP QUIZ

What is a moonlet?

ⓐ a group of moons
ⓑ a small moon

KEY WORDS

- shout
- spend + *Time* + *Verb*-ing (spend-spent-spent)
- count
- difficult

- at last
- in total
- mconlet
- enough

"I am the flattest planet," said Saturn.

"You do look a bit squashed," squeaked Mercury.

"I also have another name," Saturn went on.

"Thousands of years ago, there were people on Earth who studied the stars.

They called me 'Lubadsagush.'"

Mercury squealed with laughter.

"What a silly name!"

"It means 'oldest of the old' or 'oldest of the old sheep,'" said Saturn.

"People called me that because I seemed to move very slowly to them."

Mercury stopped laughing.

It didn't seem like such a silly name after all.

POP QUIZ

Mark T for true or F for false.

Saturn is the flattest among the planets.   T / F

KEY WORDS

- flattest
- a bit
- squashed
- thousands of years
- ago
- study
- Lubadsagush
- squeal with
- laughter
- silly
- mean (mean-meant-meant)
- oldest
- the old
- sheep
- seem
- slowly
- after all

Comprehension Quiz

A Choose the correct answers.

❶ Which planet has more moons?   **Uranus / Saturn**

❷ Which planet has more rings?   **Uranus / Saturn**

❸ Which planet is named after Greek god?   **Uranus / Saturn**

❹ Which planet is flatter?   **Uranus / Saturn**

B Mark T for true or F for false.

❶ Uranus has twenty-seven moons around it.   T F

❷ The center of Uranus is made of ice and rock.   T F

❸ The atmosphere of Uranus is made of gases.   T F

❹ The moons of Uranus do not have names.   T F

C Choose the best answer to each question.

❶ Why is Uranus known as an ice giant?

a) It is entirely made of ice.

b) Its core is only made of ice.

c) The thick layer below the surface is made of ice.

d) Its atmosphere is made of ice.

❷ Why did Saturn spend such a long time to count his moons?

a) Saturn did not know how to count.

b) There were so many moons to count.

c) Saturn did not want to answer the question.

d) Saturn was so old that he had forgotten the exact number of moons.

❸ How far do Saturn's rings stretch out on either side of the planet?

a) 30 km

b) 120,000 km

c) 120,000 m

d) 150 m

Jupiter and Mars

"Is it my turn yet?" grumbled Jupiter.

"After all, I am the biggest planet of us all."

It was true.

Over 1,000 Earths would fit into Jupiter.

"Come on then, Jupiter," said Mars, who liked to argue and fight.

"I am your neighbor.

Tell me some other ways in which you are better than me."

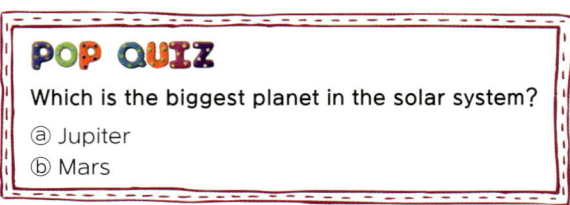

POP QUIZ

Which is the biggest planet in the solar system?

ⓐ Jupiter
ⓑ Mars

KEY WORDS

- yet
- grumble
- fit

- Come on
- fight (fight-fought-fought)

"My mass is so great that humans can't imagine the number." boomed Jupiter.

"Think of a billion kilograms.

Then multiply it by a million."

Mars tried to think of something so huge.

"Then multiply it by a million again," said Jupiter.

"And then multiply it by another million."

"Stop, stop!" said Mars.

"You're still talking about your mass.

Tell us something else."

Aha!

KEY WORDS

- mass
- great
- human
- imagine
- boom
- billion

- kilogram
- multiply A by B
- million
- try to + *Verb*
- something else
- for a while

- nothing
- a lot
- quite
- far

42 • Chapter Three

Jupiter thought for a while.

"I have over sixty moons."

"That's nothing," said Saturn.

"I have a lot more than that."

Jupiter thought again.

"My surface temperature is -108°C."

"That's quite cold," said Uranus and Neptune, "but we are far colder than that."

Jupiter thought again.

"I have four rings."

The other planets all laughed.

They knew that Saturn had a lot more rings than that.

"Those facts are not very impressive," said Mars.

"I know!" said Jupiter at last.

"I turn on my axis more quickly than any of you."

"Turn on your axis?" asked Mercury.

POP QUIZ

Which planet has more rings?

ⓐ Jupiter

ⓑ Saturn

KEY WORDS

- turn on one's axis
- quickly
- hour
- only
- minute
- fast

44 • Chapter Three

"What does that mean?"

"It means I spin around," said Jupiter.

"You all do it, too.

It takes Earth twenty-four hours to spin around once.

It only takes me nine hours and 55 minutes."

"That is fast," agreed Mars.

"This means that I am spinning very, very quickly," said Jupiter.

"I spin so quickly that all the clouds around me make beautiful patterns.

They change all the time.

Earth people like to look at them through their telescopes."

"That's true," said Earth, proudly.

"My people are so clever!"

"I don't mean to be rude, Jupiter," said Venus, "but you have a huge red spot."

"I do," said Jupiter.

"It's very famous."

KEY WORDS

- pattern
- change
- all the time

- through
- telescope
- rude

- spot
- famous

46 • Chapter Three

"Are you ill?" asked Venus.

"Do you have any cream to put on it?"

"It's not that kind of spot!" roared Jupiter.

"It's an enormous storm.

It has been raging for 350 years and it's much larger
than Earth!"

Jupiter turned to Mars.

"Beat that if you can!"

KEY WORDS

- ill
- cream
- put on (put-put-put)
- that kind of

- roar
- enormous
- rage
- much

- larger
- turn to
- **beat** (beat-beat-beaten)

Mars was ready for a battle.

"Humans named me after the god of war!" he boasted.

"Bits of rock shoot away from me and go into space.

They travel around for millions of years.

Then, some of them land on Earth!

They are called 'meteorites.'"

The other planets all looked at Earth.

"Is that true?" they said.

"Yes, it is true," said Earth.

"Meteorites come from different parts of space.

But we do have some from Mars."

▲ meteorites hitting Earth

"The people of Earth used to be afraid of me," laughed Mars.

"They thought that creatures called Martians lived here. Some of them wrote books about it.

They thought that Martians might invade Earth."

"That is true," said Earth, proudly.

"My people have good imaginations.

Did I tell you that they are also very clever?"

The other planets groaned.

"Yes, you did."

KEY WORDS

- be ready for
- battle
- war
- bit
- **shoot** (shoot-shot-shot)
- go into
- space
- land on
- meteorite
- **come from** (come-came-come)

- part
- used to + *Verb*
- be afraid of
- creature
- Martian
- live
- **write** (write-wrote-written)
- invade
- imagination
- groan

"My people have sent spacecraft to Mars," said Earth.

"They know what the surface of Mars looks like."

"They do?" Mars was surprised.

"So that's what those machines were.

They took pictures of me and they collected some of my rocks.

I didn't give them permission to do that!"

"You're going red," said Venus.

"I'm always red!" roared Mars.

"The Earth people from China used to call me 'fire star.'"

"You're certainly fiery," muttered Earth.

"I don't like being your neighbor."

"If you're so good, Earth, tell us about yourself," snapped Mars.

"But please don't tell us how clever your people are."

KEY WORDS

- always
- China
- fiery
- mutter
- oneself
- please

 Chapter Three **Comprehension Quiz**

A Circle the right word for each underlined part.

❶ The (<u>mass</u> / length) of Jupiter is so great that humans can't imagine the number.

❷ The temperature at the (<u>core</u> / surface) of Jupiter is -108°C.

❸ Jupiter has four (<u>rings</u> / moons).

❹ Jupiter takes almost ten (<u>hours</u> / days) to turn on its axis.

B Mark T for true or F for false.

❶ Jupiter has over sixty suns.　　　　　　　　　　　T　F

❷ Jupiter is colder than Uranus.　　　　　　　　　　T　F

❸ It takes Jupiter nine hours and 55 minutes to spin around once.　　　　　　　　　　　　　　　　　　T　F

❹ Jupiter has a large red spot.　　　　　　　　　　　T　F

C

Choose the best answer to each question.

❶ How do Jupiter's clouds make beautiful patterns?

a) The clouds spin quickly with the planet.

b) The wind blows them about.

c) The clouds are made of ice.

d) Meteorites crash into them.

❷ Why were people afraid of Martians?

a) They thought that Martians might be ugly.

b) They thought that Martians might throw meteorites at Earth.

c) They thought that Martians might collect rocks from Earth.

d) They thought that Martians might invade Earth.

D

Choose the correct answers.

❶ Which planet is smaller? **Jupiter / Mars**

❷ Which planet is red all over? **Jupiter / Mars**

❸ Which planet spins more quickly? **Jupiter / Mars**

❹ Which planet is named after the god of war? **Jupiter / Mars**

Chapter Four

Earth, Venus and Mercury

Earth spun around once and then began.

"I am the only planet among us to have living creatures on me." Aha!

The other planets groaned.

They couldn't compete with that.

There was no life on any of them.

"But why?" called Neptune from far away.

"Why don't I have living creatures?"

"You're too far from the sun," Earth shouted back.

"All of you, from Mars to Neptune, are much too cold."

"What about me?" asked Venus.

"And me," said little Mercury, who had appeared from behind the sun again.

"I'm afraid you're both too hot," said Earth.

KEY WORDS

- among
- living
- compete with
- life
- shout back
- from A to B
- what about ~?
- appear
- behind
- I'm afraid (cf. afraid)
- both

"I am in just the right place.

I am close enough to the sun to receive light.

Plants need light to grow.

I also receive heat.

The gases in my atmosphere trap some of that heat, like a blanket.

My atmosphere keeps me warm and helps the plants to grow.

It also keeps the animals and people nice and warm.

I also have plenty of oxygen in my atmosphere.

Living things need oxygen to breathe."

▲ Earth, a suitable planet for plants and animals including humans to live on

KEY WORDS

- right
- place
- receive
- light
- need
- grow (grow-grew-grown)
- heat

- trap
- blanket
- keep (keep-kept-kept)
- warm (↔ cold)
- plenty of
- oxygen
- breathe

"You're so beautiful, too," said Venus.

"Your oceans are so blue.

You're like a jewel floating in space."

"Thank you," said Earth.

"I am the only planet with liquid water on my surface."

"You only have one moon and it doesn't have a name."
said Mars.

"That's true," replied Earth.

"But it's a big moon.

It reflects the light from the sun, so it seems to shine
brightly.

It helps my people
to see at night."

▲ a view of the moon from Earth

KEY WORDS

- ocean
- jewel
- float
- liquid

- reply
- reflect
- shine (shine-shone-shone)
- brightly (cf. bright)

"Do you have anything else to tell us?" asked Mars.
"People once believed that I was at the center of the whole universe," said Earth.
"I think that makes me the winner, don't you?
And I would like to remind you that my people are..."
"... so clever," groaned the other planets.

"It's my turn," said Venus.
"I bring pleasure to the people of Earth.
I shine brightly in their sky.
I am almost as bright as their moon.
They call me both 'Morning Star' and 'Evening Star.'"
"Some people say that Venus and I are brother and sister," Earth said.

▲ Venus and the moon

"We are the same size, and we are both made of rock."
"But Venus, you have no moon at all!" Mars said.
"There's nothing special about you."

KEY WORDS

- anything else
- believe
- whole
- universe
- would like to + *Verb*
- remind

- bring (bring-brought-brought)
- pleasure
- almost
- Morning Star
- Evening Star
- no[not] at all

Venus looked upset.

"I am named after the goddess of love!"

"But you spin around so slowly," said Mars, who was enjoying the argument.

"It takes you 243 days just to turn around once."

"We don't all need to spin around in a hurry."

Venus was getting angry.

"At least I am not covered in craters."

"I know what craters are," said Earth.
"My moon has lots of those. They are holes made by pieces of rock crashing into it."

"I know those pieces of rock," said Mars.
"They are called asteroids. They shoot about, crashing into everything."

▲ craters of the moon

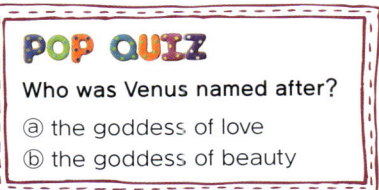

POP QUIZ

Who was Venus named after?

ⓐ the goddess of love
ⓑ the goddess of beauty

KEY WORDS

- upset
- goddess
- enjoy
- argument
- in a hurry

- get angry (*cf.* get)
- at least
- be covered in
- crater
- lots of

- hole
- piece
- crash into
- asteroid
- everything

"You do look very smooth, Venus," said Earth.

"How do you avoid getting hit by asteroids?

They are so annoying."

Venus looked out at the asteroids.

"Those great lumps of rock?

I crush them as soon as they enter my atmosphere."

Now Mars looked impressed.

"How do you do that?"

"My atmosphere
presses down on
my surface 92 times
harder than Earth's
atmosphere," boasted
Venus.

▲ asteroids floating in the universe

KEY WORDS

- smooth
- avoid
- get hit
- annoying
- look out
- lump

- crush
- as soon as
- enter
- press down
- harder

Earth gasped.

"My people would be crushed!"

"Exactly," said Venus.

"The asteroids are crushed before they reach the surface.

Nothing disturbs my smooth surface."

"You just sit there looking pale," said Mars.

"But my surface temperature is very high," snapped Venus.

"It's well above 400°C, and my clouds are made of hot acid!

So don't argue with me."

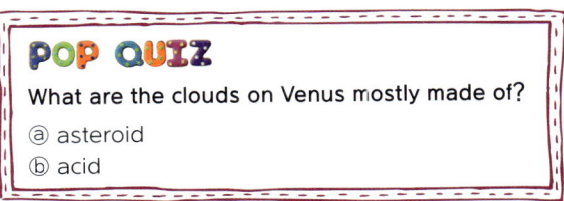

POP QUIZ

What are the clouds on Venus mostly made of?

ⓐ asteroid
ⓑ acid

KEY WORDS

- exactly
- reach
- disturb

- pale
- well above
- acid

"You have all spoken now," said the sun at last.

"No, no!" squeaked a little voice.

"I haven't had my turn yet!"

It was Mercury.

"I'm sorry," said the sun.

"I didn't see you there, hiding so close to me."

Mercury was a small, wrinkled planet who spoke in a
squeaky voice.

"I may not be much to look at, but I'm still interesting."

The sun smiled, sending out powerful rays of heat and light.

"Go on. Tell us more."

"I'm the densest planet," boasted Mercury.

"That's because I'm made of heavy metals and rock."

"That sounds like a type of music," laughed Earth.

"Some of my people love it."

"What does 'dense' mean?" called Mars.

"It means that I'm the heaviest for my size," explained Mercury.

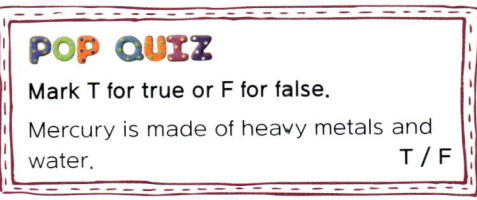

POP QUIZ

Mark T for true or F for false.

Mercury is made of heavy metals and water.   T / F

KEY WORDS

- **speak** (speak-spoke-spoken)
- **hide** (hide-hid-hidden)
- wrinkled
- squeaky
- send out
- powerful

- a ray of ~
- densest
- heavy metal
- a type of
- heaviest

"There's something I don't understand," said Venus.

"You're closer to the sun than me, but I'm hotter than you.

Why is that?"

Mercury looked at the sun.

"I don't know the answer to that.

Can you explain?"

"Of course," said the sun.

"Venus has an atmosphere that is filled with gases.

Those gases trap the heat, in just the same way that happens on Earth.

You, my little Mercury, have almost no atmosphere.

So although you are very close to me, the heat reflects off you and goes away into space."

"See?" said Mercury to the other planets.

"I told you I was interesting!"

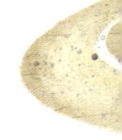

KEY WORDS

- **understand** (understand-understood-understood)
- **closer**
- **hotter**
- **answer**
- **of course**

- be filled with
- happen
- although
- go away

 A Mark T for true or F for false.

❶ Earth is the only planet to have liquid water on its surface. T F

❷ Earth has several moons, each with its own name. T F

❸ Earth is at the center of the universe. T F

❹ Earth is the same size as Venus. T F

B The following sentences are the reasons why living things can live on Earth. Put the sentences in order.

❶ Heat travels through space to Earth.

❷ Earth's atmosphere traps the heat.

❸ The sun gives off heat.

❹ Earth stays warm enough for living creatures.

_____ → _____ → _____ → _____

C Choose the best answer to each question.

❶ Why didn't the sun see Mercury?

a) Mercury is the furthest planet from the sun.

b) Mercury is always hiding behind Earth.

c) Mercury is small and very close to the sun.

d) Mercury is always covered by clouds.

❷ What did Earth say the heavy metal that Mercury talked about was similar to?

a) a type of story

b) a type of living creature

c) a type of music

d) a type of planet

❸ What is the reason Venus is hotter than Mercury even though Mercury is closer to the sun?

a) Mercury is further away from the sun.

b) Mercury has almost no atmosphere to trap heat.

c) Mercury is made of ice.

d) Mercury has no craters on its surface.

Chapter Five

Who's the Winner?

Now that everyone had spoken, the sun shone hot and bright.

The sun began to speak in a loud voice.

"Together we are called the solar system.

That's all of you planets, moons, asteroids and space dust.

Solar means sun!

It means me!

Without me, you would float away into space."

KEY WORDS

- everyone
- in a loud voice (*cf.* loud)
- without
- float away

- pull away from
- get away
- because of
- gravity

"I don't believe it," said Neptune.

"I can float away into space any time I like."

"Just try it," said the sun.

Neptune tried and tried to pull away from his orbit.

He tried to float away from the sun, but he could not do it.

"Why can't I get away?" he said.

"It's because of gravity," said the sun.

"Gravity?" shouted some of the planets together.

"What is gravity?"

The sun smiled.

"Gravity is an invisible force.

You all have some gravity."

"Yes, that's true," said Earth.

"Gravity holds things onto my surface.

Without gravity, everything would float away."

"Yes, that's right," said the sun.

"The greater your mass, the more gravity you have."

"I have the greatest mass of all the planets," said Jupiter.

"That means I have the strongest gravity."

"Yes," said the sun.

"That means that it is harder for objects to get away
from you.

But it's not as strong as my gravity."

KEY WORDS

- invisible
- force
- hold (hold-held-held)
- the greater ..., the more ~
- greatest
- strongest
- object

"Do you mean that your gravity holds us all in place?" asked Mercury.

"That's right," said the sun.

"My gravity is stronger than any of yours."

"Tell us some more things about yourself," said Mercury.

"I am very, very hot," boasted the sun.

"Hotter than any of you. My surface is the coolest part, and even there the temperature is almost 6,000˚C.  My hot center is 15 million ˚C!"

▲ the surface of the sun

"No wonder I feel so hot all the time," said Venus.

"I am also bigger than any of you," said the sun.

The planets, moons and asteroids had to agree.

The sun was 1.4 million km in diameter.

This was far bigger than any of them.

Even giant Jupiter looked tiny next to the sun!

KEY WORDS

- no wonder
- bigger
- diameter
- tiny
- next to

"Without me, you would all be covered in ice," said the sun.

"Brrr," said Venus, with a shiver.

"I give you all the heat you need.

I'm a star, so I give off light," said the sun.

"Without me, you would all be completely dark.

There would be no life in the solar system."

"I wouldn't like that!" shouted Earth.

"Plants, animals and people are what make me so special."

▲ The daytime on Earth is made possible by the existence of the sun.

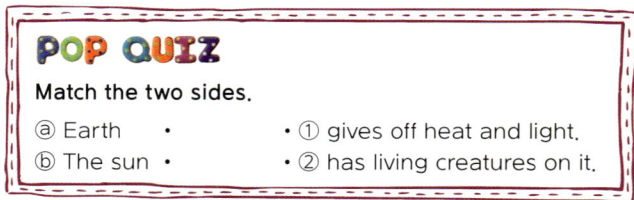

POP QUIZ

Match the two sides.

ⓐ Earth •　　　• ① gives off heat and light.

ⓑ The sun •　　　• ② has living creatures on it.

KEY WORDS

- shiver
- give off
- completely
- the rest
- family

"Do you know what I think?" said Jupiter.

"I think the sun really is the superstar of the solar system, after all, the rest of us are not stars at all.

But we are all important.

We all orbit around the sun.

Without us, there would be no solar system."

"That's true," agreed Earth.

"We're like a family."

"Are we the only solar system in the universe?" asked Mercury.

The sun laughed a great warm laugh.

"No, no.

There are billions of solar systems.

Too many for anyone to count.

And each solar system has a group of planets orbiting a star, just like me."

"Do any of the planets have living creatures?" asked Earth.

"Nobody knows," said the sun.

"But they might."

"So how big is the universe?" asked Mercury.

"Nobody knows how big it is," replied the sun.

"Nobody can even imagine how big it is."

"Some of my scientists believe that it is getting bigger every day," said Earth.

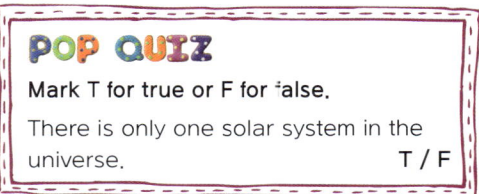

POP QUIZ

Mark T for true or F for false.

There is only one solar system in the universe.   T / F

"Do you know what I think?" said the sun.

"I think that none of us are really that important after all."

And the other planets had to agree.

The sun kept on shining, giving off heat and light.

The planets kept on traveling around and around the sun.

But when they gazed out at the billions of stars in the sky, they felt very small indeed.

And none of them ever boasted again.

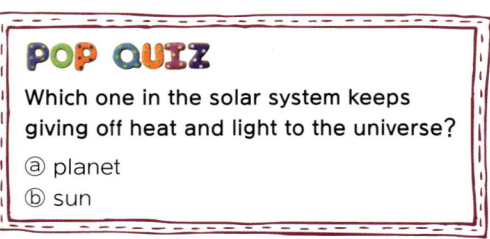

POP QUIZ

Which one in the solar system keeps giving off heat and light to the universe?

ⓐ planet
ⓑ sun

KEY WORDS

- none
- keep on + *Verb*-ing
- gaze out
- indeed
- ever

A Fill in each blank with the right word below.

traveling	shining	planets	living

❶ Each solar system has a group of _____ orbiting a star.

❷ Earth is the only planet that has _____ creatures on it in our solar system.

❸ The planets in our solar system are always _____ around the sun.

❹ The sun keeps _____, giving off heat and light.

B Circle the right word for each underlined part.

❶ There are eight planets in our (<u>universe / solar</u>) system.

❷ Without the sun, the planets would be completely (<u>dark / bright</u>).

❸ Scientists believe that the (<u>universe / sun</u>) is getting bigger every day.

❹ The planets agreed that none of them were very (<u>important / invisible</u>) after all.

C Choose the best answer to each question.

❶ Why could Neptune NOT get out of the solar system?

a) The sun's gravity was too strong.

b) Neptune was too heavy.

c) The other planets held onto Neptune.

d) Neptune's gravity was too strong.

❷ Why did the sun say that none of the planets are very important?

a) None of them have living creatures.

b) There are billions of solar systems in the universe.

c) Stars are more important than planets.

d) None of them have moons.

D Mark T for true or F for false.

❶ There is only one solar system in the universe. T F

❷ Every solar system has a planet at the center. T F

❸ The sun is a star. T F

❹ Without the sun, our solar system would not exist. T F

Let's Review the Story

Fill in the blanks to review the story.

Title: _____ System Superstar

The eight planets in our solar system are:

M_____ , V_____ , E_____ , M_____ , J_____ ,
S_____ , U_____ and N_____ .

Event:

The eight planets and the sun want to find out who is the real

s_____ of the solar system.

Question	Answer
Which planet is named after a Greek god?	
Which planet is the furthest from the sun?	
Which planet is the closest to the sun?	
Which planet is the biggest?	
Which planet has living creatures on it?	
Which planet has the most beautiful rings?	
Which planet is called 'fire star'?	
Which planet has an atmosphere that crushes asteroids?	
Which one is hotter and bigger than any of planets?	

Let's Think & Talk

Think about the following questions and answer them freely.

❶ Tell us what new information you learned about the eight planets and the sun by reading this book.

❷ It is known that there are countless other solar systems like ours in the universe. Imagine and talk about what those other solar systems might be like.

❸ If you participated in the *Solar System Superstar Contest* as a planet, which planet would you want to be? Among the characteristics of your planet, which one would you want to show off?

Let's Review the Story

Title: **Solar** System Superstar

The eight planets in our solar system are:

Mercury , Venus , Earth , Mars , Jupiter ,
Saturn , Uranus and Neptune .

Event:

The eight planets and the sun want to find out who is the real

superstar of the solar system.

Question	Answer
Which planet is named after a Greek god?	Uranus
Which planet is the furthest from the sun?	Neptune
Which planet is the closest to the sun?	Mercury
Which planet is the biggest?	Jupiter
Which planet has living creatures on it?	Earth
Which planet has the most beautiful rings?	Saturn
Which planet is called 'fire star'?	Mars
Which planet has an atmosphere that crushes asteroids?	Venus
Which one is hotter and bigger than any of planets?	Sun

Smart Readers: **Wise & Wide**

After-reading **Test**

- Solar System Superstar
- Level 3
- 23 Questions

(Vocabulary 4 / Reading Comprehension 16 /

Sentence Structure & Grammar 3)

1. Which of the following is similar to the word "invade"?

   ① groan   ② attack
   ③ change   ④ remove

2. Which one is the closest to the meaning of "invisible" in the following sentence?

   Gravity is an invisible force.

   ① can't be seen
   ② is very hot
   ③ holds things together
   ④ comes from space

3. Which pair has the wrong past tense form of the listed verb?

   ① find – found   ② know – known
   ③ spend – spent   ④ fight – fought

4. Which of the following explains the meaning of "boast" best?

   ① to talk quietly
   ② to talk loudly
   ③ to talk too proudly
   ④ to talk to each other

5. What is NOT right about the moon?
   ① It goes around Earth.
   ② It is round like a planet.
   ③ It goes around the sun.
   ④ It has lots of craters.

6. Why is Neptune so cold among the planets?
   ① It is a long way from the sun.
   ② It is blue.
   ③ It is made of water.
   ④ It has fourteen moons.

7. What is NOT right about Uranus?
   ① It was named after the Greek god.
   ② There are clouds and storms in its atmosphere.
   ③ It has four rings.
   ④ It has twenty-seven moons.

8. Who was Shakespeare?
   ① He was an astronaut.
   ② He was a scientist.
   ③ He was a writer.
   ④ He was a Martian.

9. What did Saturn boast its biggest specialty was?

① It is the roundest planet.

② It has lots of beautiful rings.

③ It is bigger than Jupiter.

④ It has some cute moonlets.

10. What is NOT right about Saturn?

① It is the flattest planet.

② People from Earth called Saturn "Oberone."

③ It's difficult to say exactly how many moons there are.

④ Rings are made of chunks of ice and dust.

11. What is right about Jupiter?

① It has a lot more rings than Saturn.

② It is the biggest planet in our solar system.

③ It spins around more slowly than Earth.

④ It cannot be seen to Earth people through the telescopes.

12. What is the red spot on the surface of Jupiter?

① a crater

② a meteorite

③ a volcano

④ a storm

13. How do humans know what the surface of Mars looks like?
① They have read books about it.
② They have asked Martians about it.
③ They have sent spacecraft to take pictures of it.
④ They have looked at it through a telescope.

14. Why is Earth the only planet in the solar system that supports life?
① The other planets are too cold or too hot.
② The other planets are too big or too small.
③ The other planets are the wrong color.
④ The other planets don't have gravity.

15. What does Earth receive from the sun?
① light and oxygen
② heat and gases
③ light and heat
④ heat and water

16. What are "craters"?
① pieces of star that fly around in space
② clouds that spin around with a planet
③ lakes of acid on a planet's surface
④ holes made in a planet's surface by asteroids

17. Why does Venus have no craters?

① The pressure in the atmosphere crushes the asteroids.

② The acid clouds destroy the asteroids.

③ The heat of the sun melts the asteroids.

④ There are no asteroids near Venus to make craters.

18. Which planet has the strongest gravity?

① Earth   ② Neptune

③ Jupiter   ④ Mercury

19. What is a solar system?

① a group of stars that orbit a planet

② a group of planets that orbit a star

③ a group of asteroids that orbit a moon

④ a group of moons that orbit a planet

20. What is NOT right about the sun and the solar system?

① The sun is the hottest object in the solar system.

② The sun is the biggest object in the solar system.

③ The sun is the fastest moving object in the solar system.

④ The sun is the brightest object in the solar system.

21. Choose the wrong part of the sentence.

> You can't be as colder as me.
> ①   ② ③ ④

※ Choose the correct sentence. (22~23)

22. ① I am the only planet among us had to living creatures on me.
   ② I am the only planet among us have living creatures on me.
   ③ I am the only planet among us to have living creatures on me.
   ④ I am the only planet among us to having living creatures on me.

23. ① You do to look very smooth, Venus.
   ② You do look very smooth, Venus.
   ③ You does look very smooth, Venus.
   ④ You to do look very smooth, Venus.

Memo

Memo

Sarah J. Dodd

Sarah J. Dodd is an experienced primary school teacher who resides in the UK, but has also lived and taught in Australia. She has a PhD in Science and a certificate in Creative Writing. She has published several books for children: "An Angel Anyway" (Anyway Press, 2008), the "Little Angels" series (Lion Children's Books, 2009/10), "The Lion Picture Bible" (Lion Children's Books, 2015) and "Legs: the tale of a meerkat lost and found" (Lion Children's Books, 2015). Her poetry for children has also been highly commended and published in the anthology "Let in the Stars" (Manchester Metropolitan University, 2014).

She is currently working on further picture books for the very young, and a novel for older children.

 Smart Readers Wise & Wide **3**-6

Solar System Superstar

Written by Sarah J. Dodd
Illustrated by Gyeonga Jeong

First Published in March 2016

Editorial Manager: Juyon Choi
Editors: Jiyeong Park, Kyunghee Jang
Designers: Eunhee Lee, Elim
Cover Designer: Eunhee Lee

Published and distributed by

 Happy House

Darakwon Bldg., 64-1 Jandari-ro, Mapo-gu, Seoul, Korea 04031
Tel: 82-2-736-2031(ext. 250)   Fax: 82-2-732-2037
Homepage: www.ihappyhouse.co.kr
Publisher: Kyudo Chung

ISBN: 978-89-6653-292-6 18740 / 978-89-6653-156-1 18740(set)

[Components]
• 1 Audio CD (Recording Studio: Aram)
• Answer Keys & Korean Translation: Free download at www.ihappyhouse.co.kr